lullabies for warriors

harleen bhogal

First edition 2021

Cover design by Niti Marcelle Mueth
Author photograph by Shin Ling Low
Book design by Annum Shah

ISBN 978-1-7776167-0-0 (paperback)
ISBN 978-1-7776167-1-7 (ebook)

stormcalledharleen.com

for jasmeen, my flower

note to the reader

these poems are vibrations more than they are words, and were
initially conceived as spoken word poetry. you are invited to
read these poems out loud, if it suits you.

this book covers topics that include: depression, anxiety,
addiction, suicidal ideation, chronic pain, rape culture, abuse
and systemic violence. you are encouraged to take care of
yourself as you read through this collection.

"If you're in pitch blackness, all you can do is sit tight until your eyes get used to the dark."

– Haruki Murakami, *Norwegian Wood*

prologue

here i build my house
at the edge where coast meets water
because even though it will soon
be carried away by the raging sea
i like
the sound of the waves

my house is temporary
i built it for the storm

the sound of thunder in the distance
is deafening
and i don't want to look outside
into the night's shadows
although i'm sure
they are more beautiful than light.

my roof is leaking
i try to patch up the cracks as much as i can
other days i let the water drench me
and i know this is no way to clean myself
i'm so sorry, i repeat
i'm so sorry

i can't tell you in words
how cold it is
but i tell myself that i am surviving

my body feels fragile, it feels weak
i hate that
yet somehow it bears this cold with such resilience
it surprises me
must be resilience i inherited

(my mother was a warrior in the cold
but that didn't stop her from hating it)

the storm continues to pass through
at the edge of the coast
where water meets sand
my house somewhere in between
i wonder what i am waiting for
if it will ever come
or if i will have to leave before it does
my house is temporary
after all.

the walls are starting to weaken
i wonder how many days have passed
time is a concept trapped in memory
but that is something i admire
about this house
in this storm of darkness and noise
i am trapped inside a timeless box

the wind is starting to pass through
i have no windows
but now the walls are starting to feel transparent
and i am starting to see through them
this will not do

so i rebuild

even a temporary house needs maintenance.

*

let me tell you about my candle
yes, there is a candle
i hold it in my hand
even as i work on my house
it is strong and it is gentle
so tranquil in this storm

on days i am drunk from its radiating warmth,
days when i am too tired to tend to my house,
i wonder where the light came from
if it was sent from the heavens
or if it was ignited
deep from the earth below my feet

some days i think of it as my rose
i protect it with my body
from the drops of cold water leaking through my roof
and from the winds
that always seem to find the cracks in my walls
my candle flickers
with aggression sometimes
but it never seems to dwindle

i always come to realize that my candle takes care of me
on days i cry into the earth
my body breaking into the dirt
one arm stretched out in front of me
from instinct, reaching out
the other holding the candle
that somehow keeps my heart warm,

how does it manage to do that?

*

my house is temporary

i patch up my roof
build more layers for my walls
but soon i will be gone
my candle keeping me warm
keeping me safe
keeping me focused

let me tell you about resilience

it only lasts as long as your mind does
it only gives as much as your body does
yet my candle does not demand me to be strong
does not demand my determination
i cry into it tears of madness
cries of desperation
defeat from a storm that never seems to pass
it gives colour back to me
pours it into my eyes
into my chest
into my feet
never receding

can you imagine a light like that?

in a storm of darkness and noise
in this temporary house

can you imagine a love like that?

part I: the storm

run hard and run fast, girl

it's not safe here

my father used to say:
brown skin is tough,

        so it doesn't easily burn.

– shield

i was six years old
when i first learned
that they will ask my body for more
than it has the capacity to give

and that they will find a way
to take it
from me anyway

hide the pain
hide the tears
no one will sit with you
if you don't stop crying

– stigma

my mother gave birth to me on a snowy night
on christmas day
1991

for twenty-one years, she fed me
looked after our home
bought all the household necessities
before they ran out

still, i knew her absence well
since i was a child
i knew that mother lived with us
but her spirit lived elsewhere
some days i wonder if it lived at all.

many years later i ask my mother's sister
if she ever felt the same way about
my grandmother
she tells me that grandmother's soul
was a fragmented one,
some parts were here and there
other parts
hadn't been seen in years

i wonder
if the other parts of grandmother
are still alive somewhere
and if those are the same parts that
have yet to give birth
to my mother

– a soul's partition

what does the term rape culture mean
to a girl who doesn't know what rape is

a girl is told it is love
before she could get a chance to know what love is

when i would devise my alter ego
i would make it white
give myself a white name
talk the way the white people talk
i knew my skin may never change colour
but in these fantasies
i turned pale
until there was no
sign of my own blood
left in me

– assimilation

i knew how to love before i knew how to breathe

– daughter

you think
that if you change
the reality you have control over
the memories
will erase themselves

denial is such a powerful kind of superstition

some days he tells me he doesn't love me anymore

i apologize without understanding what i'm apologizing for

– father

the pain starts
at the base of my spine
and sends its vibrations
through every nerve
of my body

it wants to be heard

how do i tell my body
to break intentionally
to hurt sensibly
to feel rationally

my body's muscles
are making melodies
like guitar strings
until my ground
feels like it is strumming
its existence with me
music that is not beautiful
but that is honest

the universe is riding my waves

it is listening to my story

baby, please remind me
that love
isn't supposed to feel
like occupation
on my body

that my voice
my chest
bones and breath
should never be
a possibility
of collateral damage

my body has forgotten
what it means to bloom
from love
instead of
collapsing inwards
into itself
and finding new ways to shrink

what is that fire
the one burning inside your chest
the one that never sleeps?

don't let me fall in love
like a storm no more

i want to love you
river valleys
and hot springs
dewdrops
and singing streams,
a love that nourishes
my body
rather than this hurricane rain
that has you drowning
and leaves me empty

– water

i needed the moon
the way flowers need the sun
it fed me
on nights i hadn't eaten for days

i wonder what first dates
are supposed to feel like

over and over
first encounters for me
become an instinctual
reaching for the other
in an urgency that feels as if
we are battling for our survival

the first night i will spend with you
i'll want to tell you
i love you
with no intention of regret

i mean no intention of ever stopping

but it's an overspill
a tidal wave
and its only capability is to drown
i know that

still, i will want to bury myself
into your soul
dig beneath your chest
make love to every nerve in your body
that has ever felt pain
and soften it

maybe in the process
i will also heal my own
and if not, that's okay
(it's not as important).

i cannot lie naked with you for the first time
anymore
without instantly falling in love with the feel of

your sweat against my skin,
i am already memorizing the outline of your body
the sound of your moans
and every one of your whispers
that i convince myself are secrets
reserved just for me,

all the while carving through our bones
until we are left just shells of ourselves
before there is even time left to have a morning

so we sleep in.
exhausted from the unearthing of our wounds
too weak to tend to them

suddenly too broken from each other
to not spell goodbyes

hearts stripped and trembling.

– vampire

storms always come when we are least prepared

this is not our fault

they kill that part of your brain
the part that tells you that something is wrong
that you are hurting
that things are not right

so that when your body is being destroyed
and you are bleeding internally
your brain is oblivious to it

you are numb and wonder how you are showing new scars every day

– psychological warfare

and one day when they come
with their hands and with their sweat
make sure there is no one home.

to be asleep inside your own body,
my girl,
is something you need to learn early

i wake up with my chest on fire

my teeth rattle in my mouth
as if they are warning me
of a nightmare

i don't know whether it's one
from the past
or one from the future

in our drunken hysteria
we are grieving happy
does there ever come a moment
when the love feels enough?
i don't know

but for now we are loving
the only way we know how
and we are giving
into each other
some kind of life
some kind of light
and we are breathing
into the space between
your eyes and my lips
your chest and my hips
and the words
that fall out of our mouths
to form stories
feel like stars
we can hold in our hands

and just like that
we are expanding
into constellations,
tied by the feeling
that maybe darkness
is our friend after all

the same voices that keep me up at night
might also be the ones that keep me alive.
so please
don't judge my romanticization
of my demons
when some days they're the only things that
save me

dear full moon
will you please
send softer waters
my way?

memories of the abuse
turned into such treacherous things

no one told me they would eventually take the form
of dead bodies in dreams
blood on my hands

and no other feeling than disgust

you try to wash the ache away
scrub the pain from your skin

who said staying clean was easy

the breaking body requires daily tending

is it still rape,
if you run out of the currency of
courage[1]?

[1]courage - n. they say it means to say no:
She didn't say no.

are we afraid that if we look too deep into our darkness,
into our traumas
look our truths straight into their eyes
we will no longer be able to recover?
because that fire
          (we feel it from afar and we know)
can burn us to ashes

          what is this experience of being human
          being swallowed by our own truths

i scream back
at the voice in my mind
tell it that i will find the man
i have known
whom i have trusted
and he will help me
that he has cared for me

the voice cries back
you think he is your friend?
my child,
there are no friends here
only men
who see the meat on your bones

and girl,
you don't even have much of it

– arguments

he walked into
the caves of my body
and still couldn't find me

– naked

everything is fine

everyhting is fine

everyhting is fnie

eevryhting is fnie

i remember the moments
when i searched
the bed sheets
for your heartbeat

desperately trying
to find a sign
that your heart's song
existed outside
of my imagination

i still don't know
if you were ever real

believe me when i say
it is the nature of colonization
to steal
lands, peoples, histories
which are full
and violate them into
feeling empty

that is what it also does
with our bodies

breathing is a strange kind of unease
when you've only prepared to drown

i just like the sound of the rain
and my emotions
swimming around the room
instead of in my body

– hot pools

i hope you know that you will always be my sunshine

that i will never stop catching your light
collecting it in jars
and placing them in your hands
just in case you can't see it

when our light is that powerful
it can blind us into believing it's not really there

– dear sister

you have known them
your whole life

learned which voice of yours
calms their storms
tore through the armour
of their hearts
to find their secrets,
and perfected the craft of growing
under their grip

but just because you have learned
how to bear
tame
even love
those whose hearts
have been cracked
and turned violent
does not mean you deserve
a life of breathing
into the palms
of abusers

i've had many men in my bed
never felt worthy enough
for a woman

how do you make love
to the divine
how do you touch a miracle?

somewhere between first drinks
and interlocking fingers
i find our clothes piled next to
the night stand
but i do wonder how many of you
have really stripped naked for me

even in our bed
i am trying to tear through steel gates
and always find myself wondering what we are
doing in the first place
because if this is some kind of game
i am both
winning and losing miserably
i have taken off so many of my clothes
and my skin and my bones
and i'm scared of how much more
is left of me
i am down to a few organs, really
and i am asking why it is that
you just really don't know
how to give any part of yourself
and now i'm the one with nothing left
this bed built to hold us
at our most vulnerable
has now turned into the site of
my repeated bloodshed
what is there to see of us
when there's nothing left of the night
but half kisses and untold stories

my man
who taught you to be this lonely?

the end of the world
is every time you say goodnight
every time your breath leaves my lips
every moment your fingers aren't wrapped around mine

my girl
let me tell you what your hurt is made of
it is made from hands
clasped over enough mouths
and you wonder why you were born
with no appetite

let me tell you what your weight
is made of
it is made from the stories
printed and folded
so deep within your bones
they are not words
anymore
they are hauntings

let me tell you what your heart is made of
it is made from lips
and arms
and whispers that were kept soft
just for you

you ask me what our fight
is made of
it is made of shields
and screams
and fists
and dreams
of night terrors
and deep
deep
breathing

baby girl
let me tell you what your earth
is made of
it is made of sisters holding up your skies

from the water that bleeds from your eyes
eyes that have always been strong
and these waters
i know are
flowing now
dripping
from your skin
from your hair
into the ground
until the oceans are carrying your song
the sky reflects your waters
and your waters are on fire now

– the healing

part II: the sea

i live on an island
isolation like i've felt
many times before
only this time i am stranded

my island isn't very big
and i can circle its edges in a half day
it doesn't house anything living
other than its trees
which i'm sure were meant to be tall
but now they all have
broken trunks and branches
probably from the sea storms
(they are not forgiving)

when the storms hit
my priority is hiding
and this desire
this skill to hide well
comes easily to me now.

i mostly sleep during the storms
some of the deepest sleep
i have ever experienced

but when the storms are farther away
i like to watch them
the hurricanes and tornadoes
battle in the distance
and i set up my camp right
on the beach.

the show is spectacular

rain and water
coil and spiral
create dancers

in the sky
i watch their performances
and feel along

*

occasionally there are forest fires
on these days i have to run
sometimes directly into the water
holding my breath and wondering
if i will drown waiting
for the fires to go out

on the calmer, lonely days
i find solace in going for
more peaceful swims
lie on the water starfished on my back
until i feel i am part of the sky.

i often sleep in the caves
there are many of them on
this island
sometimes i hear voices inside them
they tell me stories
and listen to mine
i tell them about my homes
that one by the coast
and the others in the cities
about the city lights
how i loved them so much
getting lost in the buzzing sounds
the smell of smoke
people breathed
out of their lungs
like dragons.

the voices from the caves

tell me stories
of shipwrecks and desert heat
and of smoke from the fires
so i know there were once dragons
here, too

*

on a bright day
i wander by a sandy shore
waves screaming close by
the air gets heavy and there is fog
enveloping my limbs like it's hungry
the mist thickens
gets into my head
and into my body
effortlessly sweeps me towards
the sea
eventually i fall asleep
and end up sleeping for centuries

– coma

substitute the longing
with alcohol

no i'm fine

even with the vomiting
and the rotting insides
alcohol will still treat you
better than the men will

the depression
makes me do things
i do not want to be doing

tying myself to my bed
sedating my legs

and when they say they want to dance
i'm killing them instead

my consciousness crawls
into my heart
and sleeps there
day in and day out
it doesn't want to think anymore

you said goodnight instead of goodbye
and just to be sure i'm replaying your words
in my mind
like a child's toy train track,
the sound of your voice
growing more heavy,
somehow less steady

you said goodnight
instead of saying goodbye
so caught between hope and denial
fear and defeat
i decide that sometimes it is important
to take words
at face value

you spoke gently to me
a whisper
somewhere far above my ceiling
one moment you felt like a distant night bird
the next you were a whole galaxy

your voice was dripping
sweet coconut milk
that i was drinking
so thirsty
so deprived
as if i'd never had anything sweet
in my life

my own lips now
dry and cracking
exhausted
anxious
breaths soft
but quick and heavy
they know something has left me

how is it
that the faster you disappeared
the more strongly you consumed me

my fingers roam my bedsheets
restless, searching
i find a cork from a wine bottle
put it in my mouth and suck
not knowing why

when the sound of your voice
your lingering last word
drifts away and eventually
dissolves into the black sky,
your memories don't stop drowning me
no matter how many
lifetimes go by

– withdrawal

in this hazy existence
life feels too far
to remember what living
smells like
what it
tastes like

other days it feels
just
fingertips out of reach
no matter how close i get
it slips away

i wonder
what being fully alive
feels like

i wonder
if there is existence
outside this dull ache

even in dreams
i wonder what it must feel like
to dream

– chronic

the smell of rotting
a faint whimper

then nothing

– 4 a.m.

i sink to a depth
of depression
where any joy that manages
to pass through
the cracks
of my body

    sears the skin

i fill my veins with poison
it makes its way into my lungs
my thoughts
eventually finds home in my stomach
and the earth's forces don't compare
to the ones it erupts in the pit of my belly
until i can no longer keep them inside

i vomit
on these nights this becomes my cleanse

– purge

don't forget, sometimes stagnation is part of the growth
part of the healing

smoke out the thunderstorms inside me
with fire
turn my cries of anguish into
moans of pleasure
let me melt away into your body
as if it is actually a viable escape

how my need for a temporary fix
is strong
but when it is so sweet
it is hard to think about the ashes
that will be all
that remain
the next morning.

– addict

anything but the present
anything but this ruptured moment
this ground i am standing on
that has already shattered
so i am floating in mid-air
half living, half dying
some kind of Schrodinger's suicide
and i just hate the waiting
more than i think i'd hate hitting the ground

and i know that life can't start
before that next inhale
but breathing is only breathing
when you're no longer choosing poison
over staying awake

i want to die

hunched over bathtub walls
i am throwing up my soul
into its drain

it smells like the poison
tastes like the poison

sweat is dripping
down my cheeks
like my skin is giving
back the ocean inside me
          (it doesn't want it anymore)

the screams project
off the tiled walls

and even as my dark, black
insides
create pools of gore
against the smooth white ceramic
i am still thinking of the poison

how good it tasted
how it made me feel like
i was swimming
turned my bed
into waterfalls
convinced me
i was just bathing

i collapse into the tiled walls

the walls scream back:

drink, it feels good.

what do you do
when you reach that point
of heartache
when it makes home
in your bones

when your veins
have been flowing with
more longing
than blood

and you don't even remember
what it ever felt like
to not be missing somebody

last night i dreamt of her,
and i've been waiting to
fall back asleep
just so i can again be
in her company

to see her eyes
smiling back at me
my goodness
she could make anyone feel
like they were the most special
person in the world.

and let me tell you
she moved like water
no, wait
she *was* water
and for those moments that she let me
i sailed in her waves

now awake (and without her)
i have come to learn a jarring truth:
nothing
no one
that came after her
felt close to the way she made me feel.

and that's alright,
i am an extension of her grace
she is the earth
everything alive
breathes through her

in a hallucination
i hear my own body hit the cement
        (a moment ago it was hovering along my
        bedroom window ledge)
the sound deeper than i would have imagined
like a supernova imploding
        its destruction swallowed
        by the vacuum of space

– disintegrate

the cold of the deep waters
has spread to my mind
and like a frostbite
slowly starts to take away all sensation
so my eyes close and i feel nothing

when there is no more mind
there is no more body.

on days my vision comes into focus
all i see is a spiritless ghost
and she drifts
but she does not see
she does not feel
she cannot touch
and she can't be touched

i look around to a world that is black and heavy
but she is white
and she is weightless
and she is nobody

and i cannot ask her what is wrong
because she has no thoughts
and she has no memory

how ironic

that not wanting to be awake

makes it so impossible
to fall asleep

– insomnia

baby pull me so deep into your arms
that i disappear completely into your body
and you disappear into mine
and our pain is not pain anymore
it has nebulized into stars circling around the room
in a cosmic dance of ache and joy and longing and
feeling so full
we could die right here

funny how when i think about love
i think about
destruction

the disintegration
of our
bodies
until they are
echoes
of
other

people

entirely

the flip

let me tell you about the flip / it consumes the pit of each bone /
turns it into mud / turns it into rot / turns it into waste / it
consumes me / or rather / it turns me / inside out / inside to
outside / until my organs spill out / like stew made of nerves
and guts / my nerves and guts / deep red intestines and black
blood / spilling / spilling / spilling / until my stomach has
nothing to feel / but dry bone socket / the flip happens when
father tells me / tells me that i made a mistake / but i did not
make a mistake / i am a mistake / and he made me / oh what
a mistake / what a mistake / and father is always telling me /
even between distances / father is spilling my guts / and carving
through my bones / until i come to / and this coming to is not
any easier / but the flip happens / it keeps happening / almost
as surely as the earth orbits around the sun / father likes the flip
/ the people like the flip / it feeds people the food / that is in my
stomach

your absence caresses me
even as i dream

souls born from the same star
are never really apart
they share the same breath

no one ever told me
that every shot of whiskey in your name
can't be a prayer

sea foam waves kiss
my floating body
dance with my dreams
and i start to drift into
something
that will always be a secret from me

eventually the possessive waters
pull me deep into their mother's
belly

still in deep unconsciousness
i open my eyes and feel
the salt enter
through my eyelashes and into
my blood.

inhale

this floating
this lethargy
my bones dissolve into
my bloodstream
my blood dissolves into these waters

and i am breathing,

   i
am breathing

– mermaid

deep inside i knew what i deserved

but i feared that what i deserved
wasn't coming

tell me that love is not madness
when it feels like centuries have passed
but i can still feel
your lips devouring mine
your hands pressing into my back
with such force
i was sure i would
fuse into your body

your laugh has written stories in my mind
stories you didn't get a chance to tell me yet
but that i had already traced from
the lines on your palms
and the curves of your smile

i've missed you
        but isn't it easier to love someone infinitely
        once they are gone

somehow i still find reasons to live
        if i convince myself you're still somewhere
        beside me

when life became more sweet
the dreams became more violent
as if warning that nothing easy to swallow
ever lasts

i knew
if you stay in water long enough
your skin becomes wrinkled
but i always wondered
what happens if you stay even longer

i've been in this ocean
for too many lifetimes
i've slowly started developing scales
velvet and mystery

i learn
if you want to survive in the ocean
you have to become it

i look down at my left arm where my scars
used to be
they have been absorbed into the scales
around them
if you look closely, you can make out
that some scales are slightly different shapes
than the rest
enough so i still know where
scars used to be
but the patterns are similar enough
that even i sometimes forget the scars
were ever there

it is known
that we are from the water
born mermaids
(who one day ventured to the dirt)

our body still recognizes the salt
the weight
the spirits that breathe with water

we are of many worlds

i imagine all
our migrating bodies
star to water
water to land

all our fleeting histories

and inside our lungs
our restlessness for a home
we don't know for sure exists

– listening to the ocean

part III: the winter

this here will not be
the work of daises and
hummingbirds

this here
is an extraction

it is brutal
and it is bloody

– the recovery

when i come back to life
i start chasing waterfalls

they remind me of a forgotten story

there exists a thick blue thread
that connects loneliness
to displacement
i find a solitary village and ask its people
if there is anyone else
with my name

because love is not going to save us
that there is any kind of savior
is the most severe of conspiracies
and maybe we are both here
just waiting
to die

      in the meantime
can you even fuck the trauma out of the body
cause goddammit we're gonna try

but maybe the space where we hold each other
when we are breaking
and when we are bleeding
is enough for now
      and oh because bleeding and breaking is part of
      the healing yes this bloody healing that is always
      bloody and always brutal and always torturous
but darling your waters will run clear soon

and until they do
i'll be right here
baby
waiting for you

a snowstorm sweeps through
my village
and quickly turns into a cloud
massive and idle

during this winter
the hunger becomes more real

and the colder it gets
the more hungry i get

it manifests as a gaping hole
inside my chest
a restlessness

it crawls under my skin
until there is screaming,

it is painful
it makes me cry out
grab on to anything i can

maybe there is something i can feed on

but there's not
it only gets colder
i only grow more hungry

– empty

what does self-love even look like?
i think it looks like liberation

the heavy mist
returns one night
while i'm still asleep

stays with me for days
enters through my fingertips
and makes its way into my organs

black and dense
something i cannot touch
but that binds me

this substance that
makes my body feel like a grave
even in my fantasies

sometimes my eyes wake
and i am stuck in a paralysis

a body trapped in a mind
a mind trapped in a body

this smoke that only makes me
want so badly to vomit
but on these nights
i am not able to

you are constantly restless with fear
because you have learned
the universe's truths
and understand their magnitude

turn the screaming
inside out

your shaking is what
breaks the walls
of your human spirit
and allows it to expand.

– what it means to have anxiety

do not be mistaken
cutting yourself from her
does not reverse the transfer of history

you wonder why you ache
that dull pain in your bones
some days faint
but always there

trauma is inherited.

– mother

it's been winter for eight years
and by now everything has frozen

some days i think about what the thaw will look like
sometimes when things have been frozen for so long
you realize that after they soften
that they have gone rotten

i wonder if that also happens to people

during this chronic winter
life has become mechanic
but not in any way that makes living easier

chronic winter makes life
a chronic battle for survival
you are always
always
fighting the winter
even when you learn its nature

some days you dream about flowers
they float around you
like dandelion seeds
they always feel like magic

the flowers have colour:
deep oranges and reds and so many shades of violet
they feel warm in these dreams
you feel warm in these dreams

during this deep freeze
you don't notice how unclean you are
because even the dirt freezes
your bed
your clothes
your skin

dirty
underneath the sheet of ice

you wonder if it is spring somewhere
it must be spring somewhere
summer even

i dream about breathing into the air around me
without creating fog

– still

i wrap a strand of hair
around my fingers
like a dance and
with coconut oil on my palms
eventually move down to
caress my bare skin
which is now
glowing in the afternoon sun

i envelop every part of my body
flex each muscle
like i'm making sure it is still alive

when i am done
i stand in front of my mirror
to see what
i've spent the afternoon nurturing
but my reflection is too far from me

i drop down on to the ground
cross my legs
hunch my back
curl my neck until
my gaze has turned
inwards and i can see into the
eyes of my naked body

shame returns by habit
even long after we've rationalized
       loved
        empathized
with the parts of ourselves
we know are thirsty for it

we fall off the wagon
because it's just that easy

we get comfortable
with this sense of stability
that self-hate brings us

a smooth transition between past and present
lies that are so much more believable than the truth

– cocoon

you've seen a sunset
so you know
that
things can still feel beautiful
even as they're leaving you

are we meant to feel like we are starving?

like i am feeding my body, but still i find myself deteriorating

i wonder if we remain malnourished when we eat what is not really important. when they tell us it is all we have for food

sometimes i think they are lying

my darling
what does the word 'love'
mean to you
because for me it means that
safety
is somewhere else
fists beating at my chest
hands caressing me without
my consent
safe houses demanding rent
              that i cannot pay

does 'love' mean anything to you?
because for me it's cliché

still when i see your eyes
it makes me want to stay
even if it'll hurt to stay

some days the healing of your scars will look
so much more brutal and
feel so much more painful
than the trauma that created them

tend to yourself anyway

know that you deserve to get there

– wound

i was made
from too much fire
and earth
to be your plaything

all this time
i thought i was screaming
into a void
all this time
the void was me
but in what you called a black hole
i have now found galaxies

here's to those faces
that still get touched by sunshine
every once in a while
despite not being able to feel it

as if the depressed aren't trying hard enough

as if we're not trying every day
to create spaces of softness and
beauty wherever we can

as if making our joy is not the most
powerful force in the universe

– you don't see us

i circle around the
frostbitten lake

dust of snow and ice
emitting from the surface of the frozen
water like flames

ice is its own fire

the flames play with the sun's rays
as if teasing this fire goddess
of the sky

even the footprints i leave
behind me are fleeting
playing with the wind.

this alluring peace
          this unexpected safety

i breathe in ice air
melt it into honey

one day i meet someone
who is just as skin hungry as me

we reach at each other's warmth
like all the monsters that we've seen
are again circling us like vultures
but this time it is us who are scavenging

every night we come home
we devour each other

and for the first time
having feasts made of our bodies
doesn't feel like a violent thing

the sun
this new optimistic sunshine
falls gently on my cracked skin

the ground below me feels
calmer than i am used to

there's a branch hanging low
and i pick off a bud and play with it
roll it between my fingers
until it dissolves into wet
green dye

people around me
are wearing lightweight skirts
and their hair is dancing in the breeze

i wonder if anyone is experiencing this spring
while there are still snowstorms inside them

and if they are
what do they make of the crashing of
cold and warm
that turns into mist
and disappears

– cycles

and girl let me tell you
that coming home
isn't really about coming home
more than it is about building one.

– begin

i am standing at the train station
        announcements blaring through the speakerphone
      i am at the edge of the train track platform
the sky looms grey   heavy   and i feel grey and heavy

a bellowing white train approaches in the distance
          and i know it's not coming to hit me
but somehow it still feels   like every train is coming to hit me
feels like every train is hitting me
        has hit me   will hit me

i feel the pain of the crash being momentary and then a release
my soul rises   gently   softly   without urgency
    out of my body   hangs there
glowing

my soul
hues of gold, the colour of the womb i birthed from

it floats   it has no blood left   no pain left
   it is weightless like how light is weightless but full

  the way my mother   and grandmother were born

  the way the universe glowed when it took its first breath.

– egg

i spend nights putting out the fire
that erupts in my house

again and again
and i don't understand where
the fire comes from

in the morning when i
leave my house i am too tired

i look outside,
and
            the world is burning

there is a difference
between wandering with
entitlement
and ascending towards
what is meant to be yours
what has always been yours

know the ground you occupy
know which once belonged to you
and which never did

your soul may be without borders
but in this world
everything is a war

know which side you're on
the history of the soil that runs through your veins
the skeletons that live inside your bones
the rivers of blood at your feet
and those mouths who drank from it
without asking

– where do you come from

my darling
may you hold yourself
with as much ease
as the sky holds the moon

look at how you caress
the brightness from the stars
and send it back to them

how lucky we are to have you

– for the young girls full of light and love

i wait for the day our bloodlines
no longer carry trauma

the day
when our children
will bleed the waters
of healed bodies

we don't have to be the answer
we are only part of the work

part of this journey

today i asked myself

what would happen if the pain inside
was felt again?
this time
without any shame
or disappointment
or envy

what happens
when pain is revisited?
this time
with the chance to hold the space
rather than be told
it is not in any way deserving

today i released the pain,
let it play
among the warm rays of sunshine
and my body thanked me by melting
into itself
and giving warmth back to me

when the fire fades into the distance
soaring back into starry darkness
give your heart to the skies
drink your tears
take a deep breath
and sing your own lullabies

your magic is a thread
which stretches out
for light years
until it reaches the infinite (edges) of the universe

you still don't believe in it?

flowers are the bravest
souls i've ever met
they stay delicate no matter how many times
they have to birth themselves again
after the winter strips them
of their petals

i live inside a hibiscus flower
for the duration that my heart feels like stone,
my guardian flower sings me lullabies
until my heart melts into honeycomb

when he tells you to
go with him
nurse his heart
fill his oceans
and help him build
his empire

you tell him
you are
an empire

to be part of the people who fought for their soil for so many years
until soil itself became the essence of our being,

do you understand what it means to again be displaced

without ever having touched that soil?

to have been born on foreign land, land that itself
is lost somewhere between violence and theft
its own soil poisoned by pirates
its rivers contaminated by their greed?

i was born on the grounds of an ongoing invasion that i cannot see
on an invisible graveyard of bodies and blood
and silence

oceans away from my mothers' birthplace
where people look like me but would probably also look at me

i know,
i resemble one place
and sound like another

and i feel like neither

maybe it's okay that we weren't meant to have a home
when most homes now have been made inhabitable by invaders

maybe we can be like the wind
that touches everything but keeps nothing for itself
that cannot be held by the hands of the earth
but maybe the earth holds it in other ways

– lost and found

Acknowledgements

I am blessed with the most beautiful young souls in my family, for whom I write, dream, and breathe: Jasmeen, Rachelle, Tanya, Ricky, Karan, Mehak, Viraj, Sana, and Logan. I owe so much to Nicki for being my partner in crime, always. I am thankful always to all the powerful women who came before me, including my mother, my aunts, my grandmother, and my older sister Leena, for everything.

Sincere thanks go to all my friends, my chosen kin, who over the years have taught me everything I know about healing, loving, and storytelling and who have supported me through my writing journey. Special love and thanks to Lui, who kept me alive these past eight years and who has given me so much beauty and magic through their friendship. To Keresa and Emina for feedback on the first drafts of this book and for their continued faith in me. Thank you to everyone who cheered me on from the sidelines, I see you always.

A heartfelt thank you to my editor Inés Anaya, for her labour, dedication, and continuous support. Thank you to my graphic designer Niti Marcelle Mueth for putting so much love into the cover design. Thank you to Annum Shah for a beautiful book design.

My heartfelt gratitude to Christopher Powles, who created for me a space of learning, discovery and safety.

Thank you to this land, this earth below my feet, specifically Tiohtià:ke, and the traditional custodians of its land and waters, the Kanien'kehá:ka Nation.

Thank you to all who survived and continue to survive, and finally, all whom we have lost.

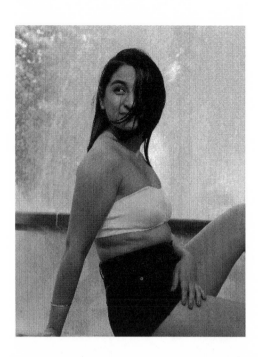

harleen bhogal is a Montreal-based spoken word performer, writer, artist, educator, youth worker, and community organizer. harleen's poetry, performance, and community work often tackle issues such as mental health, gender-based violence, and identity. She was born to two Indian parents, and often goes by her artist name **har leen**, a tribute to the Sanskrit words that make up her name and to the grandmother who named her.

stormcalledharleen.com
Instagram: @stormcalledharleen
Facebook: @stormcalledharleen